Table of Content:

CHAPTER 1:

INTRODUCTION

THE BIRTH OF ARTIFICIAL INTELLIGENCE
1.1 From Mythology to Reality: Early Concepts of Artificial Beings:

The journey of artificial intelligence dates back to ancient times, where the seeds of the idea were sown in mythology and folklore. Stories and myths from different cultures around the world often featured tales of artificial beings and creatures with human-like qualities. These mythical beings, such as the golems of Jewish folklore or the mechanical servants crafted by ancient Greek god Hephaestus, showcased early glimpses of human fascination with creating artificial life.

Moving beyond mythology, ancient civilizations also dabbled in crafting automata. Inventors in ancient China, Egypt, and Greece experimented with building mechanical devices capable of performing specific tasks. The famous mechanical pigeon invented by Archytas of Tarentum in ancient Greece and the intricate water clocks of ancient China are examples of early attempts at constructing artificial entities.

The concept of artificial beings gained further prominence during the Renaissance and Enlightenment periods. Philosophers and thinkers like René Descartes and Thomas Hobbes pondered the idea of creating mechanical creatures with human-like capabilities. These philosophical musings laid the groundwork for the development of artificial intelligence as a scientific discipline.

The concept of creating artificial beings with human-like qualities can be traced back to ancient mythology and folklore. In various cultures around the world, tales were told of mechanical or artificially crafted creatures that possessed intelligence and agency. These mythical beings served as early inspirations and reflections of humanity's desire to understand and replicate its own intelligence.

For example, ancient Greek mythology featured Hephaestus, the god of blacksmiths and craftsmen, who created mechanical servants, such as golden handmaidens, to assist him. These mythical constructs exhibited human-like characteristics and abilities, showcasing the early fascination with the idea of artificial beings.

Similarly, Jewish folklore introduced the concept of the golem, a creature made of clay or mud and brought to life through mystical means. The golem was typically depicted as a strong and obedient servant, but sometimes it also posed moral and existential dilemmas, highlighting the potential ethical complexities associated with creating artificial life.

Moving beyond mythology, ancient civilizations also experimented with building mechanical devices that imitated human actions. For instance, ancient Chinese inventors developed intricate automatons, such as the "ying zao" (shadow play) figures, which employed gears, levers, and pulleys to create lifelike movements on stage.

In ancient Greece, inventors like Archytas of Tarentum constructed the "pigeon" - a mechanical bird capable of powered flight. This early attempt at creating a self-propelled device demonstrated the ingenuity and curiosity of ancient thinkers in exploring the possibilities of artificial life.

1.2 The Dawn of Modern AI: Foundational Ideas and Milestones

The birth of modern artificial intelligence can be traced back to the mid-20th century when scientific and technological advancements paved the way for groundbreaking ideas and milestones in the field. Several key individuals and significant events contributed to the emergence of AI as a distinct discipline.

One crucial milestone was the Dartmouth Conference in 1956. Coined as the "birth of AI," this conference brought together influential figures such as John McCarthy, Marvin Minsky, Allen Newell, and Herbert Simon. The participants aimed to explore the possibilities of creating machines that could exhibit intelligent behavior. It was during this conference that the term "artificial intelligence" was coined, laying the foundation for the field as we know it today.

In the following years, researchers delved into various approaches to AI, including symbolic logic, problem-solving, and pattern recognition. Early AI systems, like the Logic Theorist developed by Allen Newell and Herbert Simon, showcased the potential of AI to solve complex problems by applying logical rules and inference.

The 1960s witnessed significant advancements in AI research, with the introduction of machine learning as a promising approach. The development of the perceptron algorithm by Frank Rosenblatt brought about a new era of AI, focusing on training machines to learn from data and make predictions.

Throughout the 1970s and 1980s, AI experienced both significant advancements and setbacks. Expert systems emerged as a dominant AI approach, allowing computers to mimic human expertise in specific domains. However, high expectations and the overhyping of AI capabilities led to what was known as the "AI winter," a period of reduced funding and disillusionment.

The field resurged in the 1990s with breakthroughs in machine learning, particularly with the rise of neural networks and the development of more powerful computational tools.

The emergence of the internet and the availability of vast amounts of data provided new opportunities for AI applications and research.

In recent years, AI has made tremendous progress across various domains, thanks to advancements in deep learning, natural language processing, computer vision, and robotics. Milestones such as IBM's Watson defeating human champions in Jeopardy! and the development of self-driving cars showcase the ever-expanding capabilities of AI systems.

The dawn of modern AI marks a continuous journey of innovation, collaboration, and exploration. The field's rich history and the efforts of countless researchers have paved the way for the transformative impact AI has on society today and the promises it holds for the future.

The formalization of artificial intelligence as a scientific discipline began in the mid-20th century, with key individuals and significant milestones shaping its emergence.

One pivotal event was the Dartmouth Conference in 1956. Led by John McCarthy, Marvin Minsky, Allen Newell, and Herbert Simon, the conference aimed to explore the possibilities of creating machines capable of exhibiting intelligent behavior. The participants discussed topics such as problem-solving, natural language processing, and learning machines, setting the stage for AI as a distinct field of study. It was during this conference that the term "artificial intelligence" was coined, providing a unifying label for this interdisciplinary endeavor.

Following the conference, researchers delved into different approaches to AI, including symbolic logic, rule-based systems, and pattern recognition. Early AI systems, such as the Logic Theorist developed by Newell and Simon, showcased the potential of AI to solve complex problems by applying logical rules and inference.

In the 1960s, the concept of machine learning gained traction, with pioneers like Frank Rosenblatt developing the perceptron algorithm. This algorithm enabled machines to learn from examples and make predictions, marking an important shift toward data-driven approaches to AI.

During the same period, researchers explored the possibility of creating programs capable of understanding and generating natural language. Joseph Weizenbaum's ELIZA, a computer program that simulated conversation, demonstrated the potential of AI in the realm of human-computer interaction.

In the 1970s and 1980s, AI research witnessed both remarkable progress and setbacks. Expert systems emerged as a dominant AI approach, allowing computers to mimic human expertise in specific domains. Systems like MYCIN, designed to diagnose and recommend treatments for bacterial infections, demonstrated the practical applications of AI in complex problem domains.

However, high expectations and the overhyping of AI capabilities led to what was later referred to as the "AI winter." The term denotes a period of reduced funding and dwindling interest in AI research, as the technology failed to live up to the grandiose expectations set forth by media and public perception.

PART 1:
Understanding Artificial Intelligence

1. Defining AI: Narrow and General Intelligence

Artificial Intelligence (AI) refers to the development of computer systems that can perform tasks that typically require human intelligence. It involves the creation of intelligent machines capable of learning, reasoning, and problem-solving. AI can be broadly categorized into two types: narrow intelligence and general intelligence.

Narrow intelligence, also known as weak AI, focuses on developing systems that can perform specific tasks or functions. These AI systems are designed to excel in a particular domain, such as speech recognition, image processing, or playing chess. They are highly specialized and do not possess the ability to transfer their knowledge or skills to other domains.

On the other hand, general intelligence, also referred to as strong AI or artificial general intelligence (AGI), aims to create machines that possess the same level of intelligence and cognitive abilities as humans. AGI systems would be capable of understanding, learning, and performing any intellectual task that a human can do. Achieving AGI is a long-term goal of AI research, and it remains an area of active exploration and development.

2. Types of AI Systems: From Rule-Based to Machine Learning

AI systems can be categorized based on the techniques and approaches used to develop them. Here are some key types of AI systems:

2.1 Rule-Based Systems:

Rule-based or expert systems use a set of predefined rules and logical reasoning to make decisions or solve problems. These rules are typically created by human experts in a specific domain and encoded into the system. The system then applies these rules to process inputs and generate appropriate outputs. Rule-based systems are widely used in areas such as medical diagnosis and decision support systems.

2.2 Machine Learning:

Machine learning (ML) is a subfield of AI that focuses on creating systems capable of learning from data and making predictions or decisions without being explicitly programmed. ML algorithms learn patterns and relationships in the data through training and optimization processes. There are several types of machine learning, including:

- Supervised Learning: In this approach, the algorithm learns from labeled examples to make predictions or classify new data. It is provided with a training dataset where each example is labeled with the correct answer, allowing the algorithm to learn from the input-output pairs.

- Unsupervised Learning: Unsupervised learning algorithms aim to discover patterns or relationships in unlabeled data. These algorithms explore the data's inherent structure and identify clusters, anomalies, or patterns without any predefined labels.

- Reinforcement Learning: Reinforcement learning involves training an agent to interact with an environment and learn optimal actions through a reward-based system. The agent receives feedback in the form of rewards or penalties based on its actions, enabling it to improve its decision-making abilities over time.

2.3 The Turing Test and the Quest for Human-like Intelligence

The Turing Test, proposed by British mathematician Alan Turing in 1950, is a benchmark for determining a machine's ability to exhibit human-like intelligence. In the Turing Test, a human evaluator engages in a conversation with both a human and a machine through a text-based interface. If the evaluator cannot reliably distinguish between the human and the machine, the machine is said to have passed the test.

The Turing Test highlights the quest for creating AI systems that can emulate human intelligence to such a degree that they become indistinguishable from humans in natural language conversations. While passing the Turing Test is a significant milestone, it is not the sole criterion for achieving AGI. AGI requires machines to possess a broad range of cognitive abilities, including understanding context, learning from diverse experiences, reasoning, and abstract thinking.

In summary, AI encompasses the development of computer systems that can perform tasks requiring human-like intelligence. It can be categorized into narrow intelligence (task-specific) and general intelligence (human-like). AI systems can employ various approaches, including rule-based systems and machine learning

3. History of Artificial Intelligence

3.1 The Dartmouth Conference: The Birth of AI as a Field

The history of artificial intelligence can be traced back to the Dartmouth Conference, held in the summer of 1956. This conference is often regarded as the birth of AI as a formal field of study. It was organized by John McCarthy, Marvin Minsky, Nathaniel Rochester, and Claude Shannon, who brought together leading researchers from various disciplines to explore the possibility of creating intelligent machines.

At the Dartmouth Conference, the attendees discussed the potential of building machines that could simulate human intelligence. They believed that "every aspect of learning or any other feature of intelligence can in principle be so precisely described that a machine can be made to simulate it." This marked the beginning of AI research and set the stage for the development of the field.

3.2 AI's Evolution: Key Moments and Paradigm Shifts

Throughout its history, AI has experienced several key moments and paradigm shifts that have shaped its development. Here are some notable milestones:

- Early AI Research (1950s-1960s): Following the Dartmouth Conference, AI researchers focused on developing rule-based systems and symbolic reasoning approaches. The Logic Theorist, created by Allen Newell and Herbert A. Simon in 1956, was one of the first AI programs that could prove mathematical theorems.

- Symbolic AI and Expert Systems (1960s-1980s): Symbolic AI, also known as classical AI, dominated the field during this period. Researchers aimed to represent knowledge and reasoning using symbolic logic and formal rules. Expert systems, which used rule-based systems to mimic human expertise in specific domains, gained popularity.

- Rise of Machine Learning (1980s-1990s): The emergence of machine learning algorithms brought a shift in AI research. Researchers began exploring approaches that allowed machines to learn from data. Backpropagation, a method for training artificial neural networks, was introduced in the 1980s and played a crucial role in advancing machine learning techniques.

- AI Winters (1970s-1980s, 1990s-2000s): AI experienced two "AI winters" characterized by reduced funding and waning interest. The first AI winter occurred in the 1970s and 1980s when early AI hype failed to deliver practical applications. The second AI winter happened in the 1990s and early 2000s when high expectations for AI were not met, leading to a decline in investment and research.

- Big Data and Deep Learning (2010s-Present): The availability of massive amounts of data and advancements in computational power led to a resurgence of AI. Deep learning, a subfield of machine learning that utilizes artificial neural networks with multiple layers, demonstrated remarkable performance in areas such as image recognition and natural language processing. This period witnessed significant breakthroughs and widespread adoption of AI technologies.

3.3 AI Winters and Resurgences: Lessons from the Past

The AI winters serve as important lessons in the history of AI. They highlighted the challenges and limitations of early AI approaches, and the need for realistic expectations and incremental progress. These periods of reduced funding and interest also led to valuable reflections and redirection of research efforts.

The resurgences of AI after the winters demonstrated the importance of breakthroughs, new approaches, and increased computational capabilities. The integration of big data, cloud computing, and deep learning methods played a crucial role in the recent AI advancements.

Today, AI is thriving in various domains, including healthcare, finance, transportation, and entertainment. It continues to evolve, with ongoing research into areas such as explainable AI, ethical considerations, and the quest for artificial general intelligence (AGI).

In summary, the history of AI began with the Dartmouth Conference in 1956, which marked the birth of AI as a formal field of study. Since then, AI has evolved through key moments and paradigm shifts, from rule-based systems to symbolic AI, the rise of machine learning, and the current era of big data and deep learning. The field has experienced periods of reduced interest and funding known as AI winters, but these setbacks have ultimately led to reflections and redirection of research efforts. The resurgences of AI have been fueled by breakthroughs, new approaches, and advancements in computational power. Today, AI is flourishing in various industries and research continues to explore new frontiers such as explainable AI, ethics, and the pursuit of artificial general intelligence (AGI).

PART 2:

Foundations Of AI

4. Machine Learning: Algorithms and Techniques

Machine learning (ML) is a subfield of artificial intelligence that focuses on developing algorithms and techniques that enable computers to learn and make predictions or decisions without being explicitly programmed. ML algorithms learn patterns and relationships from data through a training process and use this knowledge to make predictions or take actions on new, unseen data. Here are some key algorithms and techniques used in machine learning:

4.1 Supervised Learning: Training with Labeled Data

Supervised learning is a popular approach in machine learning where the algorithm learns from labeled examples to make predictions or classify new data. In supervised learning, the training dataset consists of input samples (features) and their corresponding output labels (target). The algorithm learns the relationship between the input and output by adjusting its internal parameters based on the provided labeled examples.

Common supervised learning algorithms include:

- Linear Regression: A regression algorithm that models the relationship between input features and continuous output variables. It seeks to find the best-fit line that minimizes the difference between predicted and actual values.

- Logistic Regression: A classification algorithm used to predict categorical outcomes. It estimates the probability of a sample belonging to a specific class by applying the logistic function to a linear combination of the input features.

- Decision Trees: Tree-like models where each internal node represents a feature, each branch corresponds to a decision rule, and each leaf node represents a class label or an output value. Decision trees are widely used for classification and regression tasks.

- Random Forests: An ensemble learning method that combines multiple decision trees. Each tree is built on a different subset of the data and features, and the final prediction is determined by aggregating the predictions of individual trees.

- Support Vector Machines (SVM): A powerful algorithm for both classification and regression. SVM finds the best hyperplane that separates the different classes in the feature space with the largest margin.

- Neural Networks: Complex models inspired by the structure of the human brain. Neural networks consist of interconnected layers of artificial neurons (nodes) that process and transform the input data. They are capable of learning complex patterns and relationships.

4.2 Unsupervised Learning: Finding Patterns in Unlabeled Data

Unsupervised learning algorithms are used when the training data does not have explicit labels or target values. The goal is to find patterns, similarities, or groupings within the data. Unsupervised learning is particularly useful for exploratory data analysis and data preprocessing.

Common unsupervised learning algorithms include:

- Clustering: Algorithms such as K-means clustering, hierarchical clustering, and DBSCAN group similar data points together based on their feature similarities. Clustering is often used for customer segmentation, image segmentation, and anomaly detection.

- Dimensionality Reduction: Techniques like Principal Component Analysis (PCA) and t-SNE reduce the dimensionality of high-dimensional data while preserving the most important information. These methods can be used for data visualization, feature selection, and noise reduction.

- Association Rule Learning: This technique discovers interesting associations or relationships between variables in large datasets. The Apriori algorithm is commonly used for market basket analysis and recommendation systems.

4.3 Reinforcement Learning: Training through Interaction and Feedback

Reinforcement learning (RL) is a learning paradigm where an agent interacts with an environment to learn the optimal actions to maximize cumulative rewards. The agent learns through trial and error, receiving feedback in the form of rewards or penalties for its actions.

Key components of reinforcement learning include:

- Agent: The learning entity that interacts with the environment and makes decisions.

- Environment: The external system or simulation with which the agent interacts.

- State: The current representation of the environment observed by the agent.

- Action: The decision made by the agent based on the current state.

- Reward: The feedback signal from the environment that indicates the desirability of an action. The agent aims to maximize the cumulative rewards over time.

Reinforcement learning algorithms utilize the following techniques:

- Value-based Methods: These algorithms learn the optimal value function, which estimates the expected future rewards for each state or state-action pair. Value-based methods, such as Q-learning and SARSA, iteratively update the value function based on the rewards received during exploration and exploitation.

- Policy-based Methods: Policy-based algorithms directly learn the optimal policy, which is a mapping from states to actions. They aim to maximize the expected cumulative reward by adjusting the policy parameters. Policy gradient methods, such as REINFORCE and Proximal Policy Optimization (PPO), are commonly used in this category.

- Model-based Methods: Model-based algorithms learn a model of the environment dynamics, allowing the agent to simulate and plan future actions. Model-based RL combines learning the model and using planning algorithms to optimize the agent's behavior.

- Actor-Critic Methods: Actor-critic algorithms combine elements of both value-based and policy-based methods. They maintain both an actor (policy) and a critic (value function) to guide the learning process. The actor selects actions based on the learned policy, while the critic estimates the value function and provides feedback to improve the actor's policy.

Reinforcement learning has been successfully applied to various domains, including game playing (e.g., AlphaGo), robotics, autonomous vehicles, and optimization problems.

Here are a few additional concepts related to machine learning:

Deep Learning: Deep learning is a subfield of machine learning that focuses on using artificial neural networks with multiple layers (deep neural networks) to learn and represent complex patterns and relationships in data. Deep learning has revolutionized areas such as image recognition, natural language processing, and speech recognition. Deep neural networks, such as Convolutional Neural Networks (CNNs) for image processing and Recurrent Neural Networks (RNNs) for sequential data, are widely used in deep learning applications.

Transfer Learning: Transfer learning is a technique in which knowledge gained from solving one problem is transferred and applied to a different but related problem. Instead of training a model from scratch, transfer learning leverages pre-trained models that have learned representations from large-scale datasets. These pre-trained models are then fine-tuned or used as feature extractors for the new task. Transfer learning can save time and computational resources and improve the performance of models, especially in scenarios with limited labeled data.

Ensemble Learning: Ensemble learning combines multiple individual models (ensemble members) to make predictions or decisions. Each member of the ensemble is trained independently, and their predictions are combined through voting, averaging, or weighted averaging. Ensemble methods, such as Random Forests and Gradient Boosting, often achieve better performance and generalization than single models by leveraging the diversity and collective wisdom of the ensemble.

Bias and Fairness in Machine Learning: Bias in machine learning refers to the presence of systematic errors or unfairness in the predictions or decisions made by ML models. Bias can arise due to various factors, including biased training data, biased features, or biased modeling choices. Ensuring fairness in machine learning involves identifying and mitigating biases to prevent discrimination and promote equitable outcomes. Fairness-aware algorithms and techniques aim to address bias and promote transparency and accountability in machine learning systems.

Explainability and Interpretability in Machine Learning: Explainability and interpretability are crucial aspects of machine learning, particularly when dealing with high-stakes applications. Explainable AI (XAI) focuses on developing models and techniques that can provide understandable explanations for the decisions made by ML models. Interpretability refers to the ability to understand and analyze the internal workings of ML models, making their predictions more transparent and trustworthy. Interpretable models, such as decision trees and linear models, can provide human-readable explanations, while methods like LIME (Local Interpretable Model-Agnostic Explanations) and SHAP (SHapley Additive exPlanations) offer post-hoc interpretability by attributing the model's predictions to specific features or inputs.

These additional concepts contribute to the broader landscape of machine learning, addressing challenges such as handling complex data, promoting fairness and transparency, and facilitating human understanding and trust in ML models.

In summary, machine learning encompasses various algorithms and techniques. Supervised learning uses labeled data for prediction or classification, while unsupervised learning finds patterns in unlabeled data. Reinforcement learning focuses on training agents through interaction and feedback from the environment. Each of these approaches has its own applications and methods, contributing to the diverse field of machine learning.

5. Neural Networks and Deep Learning

5.1 The Basics of Neural Networks:

Neural networks are a fundamental concept in machine learning and deep learning. They are inspired by the structure and function of the human brain, consisting of interconnected nodes called artificial neurons or perceptrons. Neural networks learn from data by adjusting the weights and biases associated with the connections between neurons.

The basic components of a neural network include:

- Input Layer: The layer that receives the initial input data, which could be features extracted from an image, text, or any other type of data.

- Hidden Layers: Intermediate layers between the input and output layers. These layers contain multiple neurons and are responsible for learning and representing complex patterns and relationships in the data.

- Output Layer: The final layer that produces the desired output or predictions based on the learned patterns in the hidden layers.

- Weights and Biases: Parameters associated with each connection between neurons. They determine the strength and influence of each connection and are adjusted during the training process.

During training, neural networks use a technique called forward propagation to compute the outputs based on the input data and the current set of weights and biases. The computed outputs are then compared to the desired outputs using a loss or cost function. The goal is to minimize the difference between the predicted outputs and the true outputs by adjusting the weights and biases through a process called backpropagation. Backpropagation calculates the gradients of the loss function with respect to the network's parameters, allowing for efficient optimization through techniques like gradient descent.

5.2 Deep Learning: Layered Networks and Feature Hierarchies:

Deep learning refers to the use of neural networks with multiple hidden layers (deep neural networks) to learn and represent complex patterns and relationships in data. Deep learning excels at automatically discovering hierarchical representations of features in the data, with each layer learning progressively more abstract and high-level features.

The deep neural network architecture allows for the development of models capable of handling large-scale, high-dimensional datasets. The additional layers enable the network to learn intricate patterns and capture subtle dependencies in the data. By combining multiple layers, deep neural networks can extract relevant features and transform the input data into a higher-dimensional representation that facilitates accurate predictions or decisions.

Deep learning architectures, such as Convolutional Neural Networks (CNNs) and Recurrent Neural Networks (RNNs), have shown remarkable success in various domains.

5.3 Convolutional Neural Networks for Image Analysis:

Convolutional Neural Networks (CNNs) are specifically designed for analyzing visual data, such as images and videos. CNNs have revolutionized image classification, object detection, and image segmentation tasks.

Key components of CNNs include:

- Convolutional Layers: These layers apply filters (kernels) to input data, performing convolutions that capture local patterns and features. The filters are learned during training, allowing the network to automatically learn relevant visual features.

- Pooling Layers: Pooling layers reduce the spatial dimensions of the feature maps obtained from the convolutional layers. Common pooling operations include max pooling, which selects the maximum value within a region, and average pooling, which calculates the average value.

- Activation Functions: Non-linear activation functions, such as ReLU (Rectified Linear Unit), introduce non-linearity to the network, enabling it to learn complex representations.

- Fully Connected Layers: These layers connect all neurons from the previous layer to the current layer. They capture global relationships and produce the final output predictions.

By utilizing the convolutional and pooling operations, CNNs can effectively extract local features while preserving spatial relationships. This makes them particularly effective in tasks such as image classification, object detection, and image segmentation.

5.4 Recurrent Neural Networks for Sequential Data:
Recurrent Neural Networks (RNNs) are designed to handle sequential data, such as time series, speech, or text. RNNs are capable of capturing temporal dependencies and modeling sequences of data by maintaining an internal memory or hidden state that persists throughout the sequence.

Key elements of RNNs include:

- Hidden State: The hidden state of an RNN is updated at each time step and serves as the memory that stores information about previous inputs. The hidden state is recurrently connected to itself, allowing the network to consider the current input along with the context from previous inputs.

- Time Unfolding: RNNs can be unfolded in time to reveal the sequential nature of the computations. Unfolding the RNN creates a chain-like structure, where each step corresponds to a specific time step in the sequence.

- Long Short-Term Memory (LSTM): LSTM is a type of RNN that addresses the issue of vanishing gradients and can effectively capture long-term dependencies in sequences. It introduces memory cells and gating mechanisms that control the flow of information within the network.

- Gated Recurrent Units (GRU): GRU is another variant of RNN that simplifies the LSTM architecture while still maintaining the ability to capture long-term dependencies. GRU combines the forget and input gates of the LSTM into a single update gate and uses a reset gate to control the exposure of past information.

RNNs and their variants are widely used in tasks such as natural language processing, speech recognition, machine translation, and sentiment analysis. They excel in scenarios where the order and temporal context of the data are crucial for accurate predictions.

In summary, neural networks and deep learning play a vital role in machine learning, allowing models to learn complex patterns and relationships in data. Deep learning leverages the hierarchical representations learned by deep neural networks. Convolutional Neural Networks (CNNs) specialize in image analysis, while Recurrent Neural Networks (RNNs) are designed for sequential data analysis. These architectures have achieved remarkable success in various domains, driving advancements in computer vision, natural language processing, and more.

5.5 Generative Adversarial Networks (GANs):

GANs are a class of deep learning models that consist of two neural networks: a generator and a discriminator. The generator learns to generate synthetic data that resembles real data, while the discriminator learns to distinguish between real and generated data. The two networks are trained in an adversarial manner, with the generator aiming to generate realistic data that fools the discriminator, and the discriminator striving to accurately classify real and generated data. GANs have been successful in generating realistic images, synthesizing music, and producing text, among other applications.

5.6 Autoencoders:

Autoencoders are neural networks used for unsupervised learning and dimensionality reduction. They consist of an encoder network that compresses the input data into a lower-dimensional representation (encoding) and a decoder network that reconstructs the original input from the encoded representation (decoding). Autoencoders are trained to minimize the reconstruction error, allowing them to capture meaningful features and reduce data redundancy. They find applications in data denoising, anomaly detection, and feature extraction.

5.7 Transfer Learning in Deep Networks: Transfer learning, as mentioned earlier, is the practice of leveraging pre-trained models in deep learning. Pre-training a deep network on a large dataset (e.g., ImageNet) allows it to learn general features and representations that can be transferred to new tasks or domains with limited labeled data. By fine-tuning the pre-trained model on the specific task or dataset of interest, transfer learning enables faster convergence and better performance.

5.8 Regularization Techniques:

Regularization methods in deep learning help prevent overfitting and improve the generalization ability of models. Overfitting occurs when a model performs well on the training data but fails to generalize to unseen data. Common regularization techniques include L1 and L2 regularization (weight decay), dropout, and batch normalization. These techniques introduce constraints or modifications during training to reduce model complexity and improve its ability to generalize to new data.

5.9 Deep Reinforcement Learning:

Deep reinforcement learning combines deep learning with reinforcement learning, enabling agents to learn directly from raw sensory inputs in complex environments. Deep reinforcement learning has achieved remarkable successes in playing games, such as AlphaGo and OpenAI's Dota 2 bot. It involves training deep neural networks to approximate the value function or policy function, allowing agents to make optimal decisions based on rewards and environmental feedback.

These additional concepts expand the knowledge on neural networks and deep learning, covering topics such as generative models, unsupervised learning, regularization, and the integration of deep learning with reinforcement learning. The field of neural networks and deep learning continues to advance rapidly, enabling breakthroughs in various domains and driving the development of increasingly sophisticated models and algorithms.

PART 3:

AI Applications & Impacts

BEYOND THE VEIL: ILLUMINATING THE TAPESTRY OF ARTIFICIAL INTELLIGENCE